REAL WORLD ECONOMICS™

Understanding
Financial
Frauds and Scams

Philip Wolny

ROSEN
PUBLISHING®

New York

For Jonatan Kaye, a true "419 letter" aficionado

Published in 2013 by The Rosen Publishing Group, Inc.
29 East 21st Street, New York, NY 10010

Library of Congress Cataloging-in-Publication Data

Wolny, Philip.
Understanding financial frauds and scams/Philip Wolny.—1st ed.
      p. cm.—(Real world economics)
Includes bibliographical references and index.
ISBN 978-1-4488-6784-4 (library binding)
1. Fraud—Juvenile literature. 2. Commercial crimes—Juvenile literature.
I. Title.
HV6691.W65 2013
364.16'3—dc23

2011052523

Manufactured in the United States of America

CPSIA Compliance Information: Batch #S12YA: For further information, contact Rosen Publishing, New York, New York,
at 1-800-237-9932.

Contents

INTRODUCTION

Imagine waking up one day to discover that your family had suddenly lost all its savings. In an instant, everything your family had taken for granted—its home, savings for retirement or college, and much more—had vanished completely.

After the initial shock wore off, you and your loved ones would have to get used to a harsh new reality. If your parents owned their own home, your family might now be unable to continue to meet its monthly mortgage payments. If you rent, you might no longer have enough money to pay next month's rent. You might need to move with relatives into less expensive accommodations in a worse part of town. Plans for you or your siblings to attend college might be postponed or eliminated altogether. Your parents' plans to retire could be compromised.

If your savings and investments are wiped out with little or no warning, your life could be changed drastically by such a tragedy. At first, it might be difficult to figure out what actually

happened. Sometimes losses are the result of market forces and fluctuations in the business cycle, such as recessions, depressions, inflation, deflation, and stock market crashes. Other times, however, they are the result of crime; your savings have been mismanaged, misappropriated, or stolen—not "lost." Unfortunately, such crimes are more common than you might imagine. Whether you follow the news, have friends or family that have been victimized, or have experienced such crime firsthand, you have probably heard of instances of financial frauds and scams. They are a growing danger in today's wired, connected world.

Criminal activities designed to steal money from people, businesses, institutions, and governments exist in many forms. They can include very simple yet effective scams initiated by telephone, direct mail, door-to-door "salesmen," or via the Internet. These target vulnerable and gullible individuals and are designed to gain relatively small amounts of money. But

Victims of Bernard Madoff's Ponzi investment scheme are pictured holding up signs during a press conference outside the federal district court in New York City on the day of Madoff's conviction.

financial crimes may also include larger, far more high-tech frauds in which individuals or groups manipulate the system to steal millions, and even billions, of dollars.

If you have an e-mail account, chances are you have received suspicious messages requesting money or personal information. You may have received phone calls or direct mail with similar unusual requests. In the news, it seems that a major financial fraud or scam is exposed weekly, even within supposedly reputable corporations, organizations, and institutions. Whether a lone criminal operating out of his or her shabby one-room apartment or a group of powerful business executives running one of the nation's largest and richest corporations, threats to the wealth of innocent people exist at many levels and in many forms. Not just individuals, but entire nations and the international financial system itself are potential victims.

In the following chapters, we will explore many of these criminal financial schemes. Some have been around since human civilizations started using money, while others are facilitated by the growing number of tools available to criminals operating on the Internet or using modern electronic banking and securities (stock and bond) trading systems.

Governments, businesses, and ordinary individuals must be increasingly vigilant to defend against more and more sophisticated schemes. In exploring how these frauds and scams work, you can learn how to protect yourself and your loved ones. Resources, both online and otherwise, exist to help you and your family guard against these growing dangers. The old sayings, "If it sounds too good to be true, it probably is," "Knowledge is power," and "Buyer beware!" are truer today than ever before. By arming yourself with some basic tools, you can avoid falling victim to the growing menace of financial frauds and scams.

CHAPTER ONE

WHAT ARE FINANCIAL FRAUDS AND SCAMS?

For as long as humans have used money, there have been those who have found ways to cheat others out of their wealth. In the modern era, the schemes that criminals have employed have taken the form of financial frauds and scams. Such criminal schemes are many and varied, ranging from the very simple to the extremely complicated and technologically sophisticated. Some frauds are easily and quickly detected, while others may take years to be uncovered, if they ever are.

What are financial frauds and scams, really? A simple definition is any activity, including a business or business model, in which one party deceives another party and thereby dishonestly gains the second party's wealth, such as money or possessions. Simple, everyday scams are referred to as "cons," named after those who perform them: confidence men (or "con men"), scammers, or scam artists. Con men gain your confidence, then repay your trust by stealing from you. More elaborate financial frauds can also occur when apparently legitimate businesses steal from their trusting clients and customers.

We will examine many types of financial frauds and scams, starting small and working our way up to some of the most infamous, notorious, and far-reaching schemes and swindles. We will also consider how modern technologies, especially the Internet, provide increasingly effective tools for scam artists.

Common, Everyday Scams

Some of the most common scams are perpetrated on individuals and employ very simple means. Criminals can easily target someone using regular mail, or via e-mail. In addition, seemingly innocent and friendly people might approach a victim in public or even show up at one's door.

One of the problems in protecting ourselves against frauds and scams is that we are often uncertain of who, really, is on the other end of a telephone call or e-mail exchange.

9

Much of our personal information is, sadly, available online. Phone numbers, e-mail addresses, and mailing addresses are often all the gateway thieves need to gain entry and begin robbing someone blind. You or your family have probably experienced unsolicited (unasked for) phone calls, e-mails, or mail—some certainly untrustworthy, and all asking for money.

Any criminal can pretend that he or she is calling from a legitimate business, such as a bank, government institution, or charity. Some victims are perceived to be "easy marks": senior citizens, the economically disadvantaged, and even teenagers or children. Even if scammers do not ask for money directly, they may be seeking sensitive personal and financial information—names, mailing addresses, credit card or bank information, Social Security numbers—that will allow them to gain access to your money or charge purchases to your accounts.

IDENTITY THEFT

One widespread problem is identity theft, in which strangers use stolen personal and financial data to impersonate others. Using the victim's name and personal identifying information, thieves may obtain credit cards, loans, and other kinds of access to cash. One's Social Security number could be used to set up bank accounts, rent an apartment, buy a house or car, or pay for Internet service or water or power bills.

Other identity frauds include obtaining medical care and prescription drugs in another person's name. Once the money runs out or the scam is exposed, the thief will simply disappear, walking away from the financial obligations, but the identity theft victim's name will still be on all those accounts, bills, and agreements. The victim will be considered responsible for the debts until—and if—he or she can prove that his or her identity had been stolen.

Many cases of identity theft involve the criminal using the victim's Social Security number, sometimes with other forms of stolen identification. Identity thieves often try to obtain Social Security and credit card numbers directly from their victims. One tactic is to pretend they are calling or writing from the victim's bank or other trusted business and that they need to verify or update the victim's financial and account information.

Criminals may have one or more pieces of a person's financial or identifying information already. These can include anything from a driver's license number to merely an address. Think about how much of this kind of personal identifying information you, your family members, or your friends submit when shopping, banking, or registering for or subscribing to any kind of service, whether online or out in the real world. The frequency with which you are asked for this kind of information by reputable organizations gives you some idea of how many places your identifying information is stored and how many opportunities this gives identity thieves. If a thief obtains even one piece of your identifying information, it becomes much easier to discover and steal other types of information and ultimately gain access to your financial accounts.

Identity theft is particularly dangerous because victims can suffer from its effects for a very long time. It may be too late to catch the culprit by the time the victim is contacted about defaulted loans or unpaid bills that he or she knows nothing about. Trying to undo the damage done can be extremely difficult and time-consuming. Even if you clear your name, background checks by employers and credit reports may continue to turn up damaging information that reflects badly upon you, years after the crime was committed and reported.

Too Good to Be True?

Scammers often fool their victims by proposing deals or business opportunities, promising a quick or easy payoff, a "sure thing." Typical scams might include someone calling to announce that a victim has won a lottery or a prize of some kind, which can be collected if you send in a certain sum of money or provide a credit card or Social Security number. Another common scam is when the criminal impersonates someone in need who promises a reward at a later time if the victim will help him or her right now with some cash.

A common form of fraud is an advance fee scam, where victims are promised greater riches in the future if they provide a fee up front. Scammers may promise victims a prize, loan, investment, or other incentive. The fraud occurs when the victim acts on this and receives little or nothing in return. This is a classic example of the old saying, "If it sounds too good to be true, it probably is." However, professional scammers are very skilled at convincing even skeptical and savvy victims that such offers are legitimate. They take advantage of the excitement that many people feel when they think they are getting a great deal or will see a huge return on a small investment.

Fraud artists are frequently very good salespeople. A stranger might call and offer a chance to invest in a scheme, underscoring that this is a "one-time opportunity" that one needs to jump on quickly. You have to "act now!" The hard sell can be very persuasive, even if the things they are saying should be raising red flags. They may try to convince you that you do not need to consult with a family member, lawyer, accountant, or anyone else before taking the opportunity. They may try to steer you away from seeking a written agreement or contract. These are all signs that there is something rotten at the core of this supposedly sweet deal. Break off all communication if any salesperson uses these persuasive tactics when trying to get you to part with your money.

Fake Charities

Con men also try to take advantage of the goodwill of strangers. Inventing a fake charity or pretending to represent a legitimate one are common frauds. A friendly telemarketer may call to collect donations for disabled veterans, the environment, or hungry children.

It may take a long time to discover the fraud because charitable giving comes with no expectation of a return on the money spent. Those who give to charities donate knowing that they won't get anything back in terms of material goods or monetary value, so how can any potential fraud be detected? Plus, a naturally charitable person is happy to give and is usually not expecting any kind of deceit in the first place.

When soliciting donations for phony charities, criminals might insist on cash-only donations or payment via other means (usually a credit card). Criminals soliciting donations will try to steer the victims away from asking for written materials or other proof that the charity is legitimate. They stress the urgency of getting the money to those in need quickly. Often they are all-too-eager to send someone to collect the donation

Betsy Gotbaum, then New York City public advocate, is shown holding a news conference to launch the city's public awareness campaign against charity telemarketing scams.

in person. By the time a check is mailed or a credit card processed, the criminals may have even escaped with a much larger "donation" than the victim agreed to—your personal financial information that can be used to steal even more money.

THE 419 SCAM, OR THE "NIGERIAN LETTER"

One distinct category of advance fee fraud is the 419 letter. Because many of these suspicious offers have originated in Nigeria, it is also known as the "Nigerian letter" fraud. The number 419 refers to a section of Nigeria's criminal law. While this particular fraud, as the U.S. Federal Bureau of Investigation (FBI) describes it, might be considered "by law-abiding citizens to be a laughable hoax," it is surprising how many otherwise smart and savvy people are duped by it and how many millions of dollars perpetrators of the 419 fraud steal annually.

This is how the 419 letter scam works: a letter or e-mail arrives from a foreign nation (often, but not always, Nigeria). The writer identifies himself or herself as a high-ranking government or bank officer seeking a trustworthy person who will accept a large sum of money that the official needs to get out of his or her country. The victim is asked to become a partner of sorts. The sender offers a stunning amount of money in exchange for the letter recipient's agreement to deposit a sum in his or her own bank account in the United States. All that is needed is for the letter recipient to provide the letter writer with his or her bank account information so that the funds can be wired to the account. Once the bank account information is shared with the letter writer, the letter's recipient has become a victim of fraud and his or her bank account is soon to be compromised and possibly emptied.

In another version, the sender claims that the recipient's long-lost relative has passed away. The recipient stands to inherit a large amount of money from this supposed relative if he or she will provide further contact information and/or bank

Signs forbidding 419 scams and other unsavory Internet activity are prominently displayed at an Internet café in the Nigerian capital of Lagos following a crackdown on such practices.

account details. The sender sometimes requests that the recipient provide blank letterhead stationary, his or her bank name and account number, and other sensitive personal and financial information, all in the interest of securing the inheritance. The sender might forward official-looking materials, such as a letter from a bank or government, or other forged documents to create the illusion of legitimacy.

At some point, the sender informs the victim that some setback has occurred that makes it necessary for the victim to immediately provide money up front: an official needs to be bribed or the recipient needs to open up a small account in the foreign bank to be eligible for the bank transfer. Victims are promised that such fees will be more than repaid when the

Reporting a Scam

People are often very embarrassed to have become a victim of a con or scam. It is natural to feel angry and ashamed if you have been tricked out of money. However, it is important to get beyond this initial embarrassment and report any such incidents to the police or other authorities. While the chances of recovering money or other lost possessions might be slim, one can at least try to prevent others from falling victim to the same scam. You may even help bring the scam artist to justice. You should also contact the authorities if someone has tried unsuccessfully to scam you, and let your family members and neighbors know what happened. Even if you didn't fall for the scam and become a victim, alerting others will allow the authorities and those around you to keep their eyes peeled for a similar type of fraud.

large sum of inherited money is finally transferred out of the foreign country. The sender will often attempt to get as much money as possible by inventing new hurdles for the recipient until the latter runs out of money or belatedly realizes that he or she is being duped.

Get Rich Quick, Work at Home

Another scam is the sale of get-rich-quick schemes, including convincing people to buy "work-from-home" kits. Once again, the main targets are often the elderly, sick, unemployed, economically disadvantaged, or disabled, including many for whom it is impossible to work a traditional job. The online ads and flyers pasted up on utility poles or on community billboards can be seen everywhere—"Earn $500-$2000 a Week at Home!"

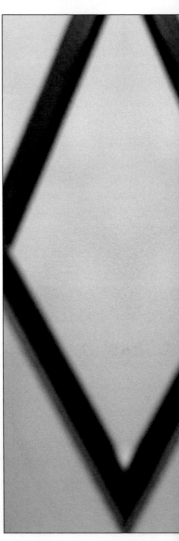

There is a wide variety of these kinds of frauds. A longtime scheme involves the victim being charged a couple of dollars via credit card to start an at-home business but then discovering that the card has been charged a far larger fee, even though he or she has never received the promised kit and materials.

The sellers can charge anything from a minimal fee to thousands of dollars for "helping" the victims set up home businesses. A housewife hoping to work in medical billing, for example, might pay the company that is selling her this expertise a nonexistent "state licensing fee." Another scam offers $1,000 a month to someone willing to mass-produce

Beth A. Silvaggi, public relations director for the Better Business Bureau of Western Pennsylvania, displays a sign warning of work-at-home scams in Pittsburgh, Pennsylvania.

19

or assemble handicrafts at home. But first, the victim must purchase a $600 start-up kit. Usually the victim then receives supplies of a very low quality. No matter how many finished handicrafts the victim returns to the company, they are rejected for being shoddy and inferior. Victims are frequently left with tremendous amounts of assembled goods they cannot sell. They have wasted hundreds of dollars and many long hours of labor and have nothing to show for it but debt.

Even worse, eager home workers may pay substantial amounts of money, only to receive instructions on how they can essentially join in on and broaden and perpetuate the scam themselves. Victims duped into paying money for the opportunity to stuff envelopes for profit often receive an instructional package that shows them how to promote the envelope-stuffing scheme to others. Similar packages are sent to victims who have inquired about online marketing opportunities. All they receive for their cash are instructions on how to place online ads that are promoting—you guessed it—online marketing!

CHAPTER TWO
PONZI AND PYRAMID SCHEMES

The desire to get a good deal is what makes individuals vulnerable to some of the garden-variety scams and frauds discussed in the previous chapter. Yet that same motivation—to get a big return with very little investment—also drives the more far-reaching and complex schemes that have made headlines in recent years. Larger financial frauds can be quite successful due to a snowball effect. Victims are often led to believe that they are getting ahead by participating in the scheme. They might experience early success, which encourages them to keep funding the scheme or stay invested in it. They may involve others in the fraud, innocently and with the best of intentions, so that thousands or even millions of people might eventually become victims.

THE PONZI SCHEME

One of the best-known examples of a large-scale scam occurred in the early twentieth century: the infamous Ponzi scheme.

Charles Ponzi, whose early twentieth-century fraud popularized the term "Ponzi scheme," is shown leaving Charlestown State Prison in Boston, Massachusetts, on February 14, 1934, where he spent fourteen years for mail fraud and larceny.

Named after the man who started it, Charles Ponzi, an Italian immigrant to the United States, it was not the first of its kind, but it defrauded more investors for more money than any similar financial scam ever perpetrated before it.

22

Ponzi, who had earlier been in trouble for other forms of fraud, including check forgery, began his scheme around 1920. This is when he discovered that there was money to be made in the trade of international reply coupons (IRCs). These coupons can be exchanged for one or more postage stamps representing the minimum postage required for the letter writer's recipient in another country to send a reply. They allow a person to send someone in another country a letter, along with the cost of postage for a reply, without first having to somehow acquire stamps from the recipient's country or send currency to help the recipient pay for return postage.

Ponzi found a way to exploit the IRC system. He discovered that a profit could be made by taking advantage of the differing postal rates in different countries. Ponzi would buy IRCs cheaply in one country and exchange them for stamps of a larger value in another country. He began offering investors incredible returns on investing in his IRC profit scheme. For example, he promised a 50 percent return, so someone giving him $1,500 would get back $750 in ninety days, with promises of continuous profits to come.

The problem was that there was no actual investment going on. Ponzi continued to attract investors and used the newer investors' money to pay out the promised profits to older investors. Because he seemed to be making good on his promise of healthy early returns on investment, the word spread and many more people grew interested and invested in Ponzi's scheme. Ponzi kept most of the investment cash that was flowing in for himself. He made as much as $20 million before he was discovered and convicted of mail fraud and other crimes. Ponzi was imprisoned for a time, and several banks failed as a direct result of his fraud.

J. David Dominelli: The Ponzi Scheme that Rocked San Diego

In the early 1980s, the city of San Diego, California, was the site of one of the biggest Ponzi schemes ever perpetrated up to that time. J. David "Jerry" Dominelli ran J. David & Associates, an investment firm based in the city's upscale La Jolla area. Because his firm claimed to deal with super-sophisticated financial transactions in the international currency (or money) markets, an unusually large number of savvy, experienced investors went in over their heads and trusted Dominelli.

Well-known millionaire investors, a famous hotel owner, and many other members of San Diego's business and society elite were among the one thousand people who suffered losses approximating $80 million when Dominelli's illegal operation

J. David Dominelli, the architect of a Ponzi scheme that rocked San Diego in the 1980s, is seen here on the right.

was finally exposed. "Jerry benefited from a lot of people who thought he was a genius," said Robert Rose, the former assistant U.S. attorney who led a two-year grand jury investigation of Dominelli, in an interview with the *San Diego Union-Tribune*.

One reason for Dominelli's success in duping so many was that he promised his clients huge early returns—as large as 40 and 50 percent of their investments. While far larger frauds have come to light in recent years, Dominelli's theft was shocking at the time. Even San Diego's mayor, Roger Hedgecock, was implicated in the scheme for accepting illegal contributions from Dominelli. After pleading guilty to four felony counts in 1985, Dominelli was sentenced to twenty years in prison.

BROTHERS IN FRAUD

The Villalobos brothers, Luis Enrique and Osvaldo, ran the Brothers Fund investment firm, based in San Jose, Costa Rica, from 1982 to 2002. One of their largest pool of clients was about 6,400 American retirees who had settled in Costa Rica. The Villalobos brothers required of clients a minimum initial investment of $10,000 to join the fund. The brothers actually paid 3.5 percent interest in cash regularly to all their clients over two decades, which was one reason why the fund did not attract complaints or suspicion for so long. The brothers also built churches, handed out free Bibles to investors, and otherwise portrayed themselves as honest, God-fearing businessmen.

All this changed in 2002, however, when Canadian and Costa Rican law enforcement officers raided the offices of the Brothers Fund and charged the Villalobos brothers with laundering drug money ("money laundering" is moving illegally obtained cash into legitimate businesses in order to throw off suspicion). At the same time, Costa Rican authorities also announced that they suspected that the Brothers Fund was in fact a Ponzi scheme. The brothers' accounts were frozen by a judge, and investigators were only able to locate $7 million.

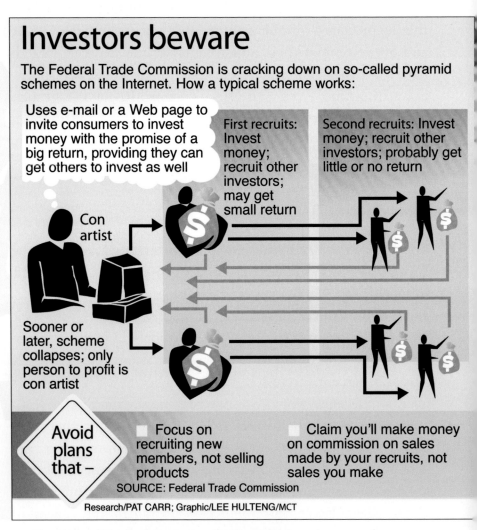

Investors beware

The Federal Trade Commission is cracking down on so-called pyramid schemes on the Internet. How a typical scheme works:

Uses e-mail or a Web page to invite consumers to invest money with the promise of a big return, providing they can get others to invest as well

First recruits: Invest money; recruit other investors; may get small return

Second recruits: Invest money; recruit other investors; probably get little or no return

Con artist

Sooner or later, scheme collapses; only person to profit is con artist

Avoid plans that –

■ Focus on recruiting new members, not selling products

■ Claim you'll make money on commission on sales made by your recruits, not sales you make

SOURCE: Federal Trade Commission

Research/PAT CARR; Graphic/LEE HULTENG/MCT

This Federal Trade Commission diagram displays the somewhat complicated and delicate set of relationships that exist in pyramid schemes. It also underscores how such frauds are destined to collapse with little or no returns to later investors.

Investigators say that most of the interest payments to Brothers Fund clients were honored through other businesses the brothers owned, while Osvaldo Villalobos allegedly ran a series of shell companies to hide the rest of the money. Shell companies are corporations whose only business is to hold money, usually to avoid tax regulations in the United States and other countries. Osvaldo Villalobos was tried and, in May 2007, sentenced to eighteen years in prison, but his brother remains an international fugitive. Meanwhile, anywhere from $300 million to $1 billion is still unaccounted for.

"One Big Lie": The Bernard Madoff Affair

In December 2008, very few people had heard of a man named Bernard ("Bernie") L. Madoff, the wealthy owner of a successful investment management business. In the hours after his arrest on December 11, however, the whole world came to know him as the criminal behind the largest stock fraud in history. Madoff's fraud resulted in the loss of billions of dollars among his investors and the bankruptcy of many ordinary people who had placed their trust and life savings in his hands.

Madoff had been a star in finance for decades, considered a genius by many wealthy clients. He produced consistent returns every year for thousands of clients, sometimes as good as 10 percent, whether the markets were up or down. Observers say, however, that this remarkably consistent rate of return should have been a red flag to investors and regulators. It was only when too many investors at one time sought to sell their Madoff investment holdings to raise cash during the Great Recession of 2007-2009 that Madoff was finally forced to admit to his fraud and face arrest, conviction, and imprisonment.

Ponzi vs. Pyramid Schemes

Ponzi schemes are sometimes mistakenly described as pyramid schemes, and vice versa. While certain frauds, especially complex ones, may actually incorporate aspects of both, they do differ. You will recall that a Ponzi scheme fools individuals, but it is always a single person or entity who is deceiving them and profiting from the deception.

A pyramid scheme, unlike a Ponzi scheme, can only continue if each person who invests then turns around and attracts other investors. The initial creator of the scheme is at the top of the pyramid. Investors are promised very high returns if they contribute, but in order to obtain these returns, they must attract newer investors with the same promises of profit. When they successfully recruit a new investor, they collect that investor's cash and give a portion of it, as a sort of commission, to the person who had recruited them. Then the new recruits seek out even newer recruits, and everyone up the chain benefits from the new investment dollars.

In this way, money keeps getting funneled up the pyramid and into the pockets of the person at the top. The scheme is destined to collapse as it grows bigger, however, because it does not generate any real income. Large profits are based, according to the U.S. Federal Trade Commission (FTC), "primarily on recruiting others to join their program, not based on profits from any real investment or real sale of goods to the public." Almost all the real money collects at the top—in the pockets of the initial con artist.

Even if a supposed product is involved (usually to throw off suspicion that it is in fact a pyramid scheme), there is generally no real money exchanged aside from the money people are paying to become part of the pyramid itself. Some law enforcement officers call Ponzis and pyramids "Peter-Paul" scams, after the old saying that someone is "stealing from Peter to pay Paul." This saying refers to situations when money is merely being shifted around, but actual wealth is not being generated.

Madoff called his investment scheme "one big lie" on several occasions. Rather than investing clients' money, he simply deposited their funds in his Chase bank account, paying out returns when needed. Meanwhile, he provided clients with fake investment reports, inventing financial transactions out of thin air, leading them to believe that their investments were real.

Other Madoff practices should have raised suspicion, including his policy of providing clients' account statements only via the mail and in printed form. Most investment managers allow clients real-time, online access to their accounts. In addition, Madoff used a tiny accounting firm in upstate New York. Many thought it was virtually impossible for such a small business to handle so many clients. At one time, the Securities and Exchange Commission (SEC) even investigated Madoff, but no suspicions could be confirmed and nothing illegal seemed to be uncovered. Victims were outraged that regulators had been blind to the fraud occurring right under their noses, especially because it seemed so brazen and obvious in retrospect. Madoff himself later admitted to lying under oath several times.

Bernard L. Madoff leaves the New York City federal court after a hearing in which his lawyer indicated the disgraced wealth manager would plead guilty to eleven counts of fraud that cost investors billions.

The size of Madoff's fraud was astounding, with estimates ranging from $50 billion to $65 billion. Victims included influential bankers; other investment funds; Hollywood celebrities like Steven Spielberg; owners of sports teams (including the New York Mets baseball team); numerous charitable foundations and organizations; and city, state, and union retirement funds, among many others. In addition, many individuals of modest means had their entire life savings wiped out.

CHAPTER THREE
CORPORATE SCANDALS

S ome of the greatest economic scandals in the recent past have taken place within, or greatly affected, giant firms with formerly impeccable reputations. The downfall of several prominent companies, and their dishonest executives, have left millions of employees and investors shocked and outraged. Many more millions of people directly unaffected by these scandals have nevertheless been victimized by the resulting turmoil in an economy and financial system shaken by the sudden loss of billions of dollars. We are all part of a national and global financial network so interconnected and interdependent that a collapse in one sector can cause shockwaves in many others.

An interconnected global economy offers enormous economic opportunities, as well as huge perils. One of these dangers is the way in which financial fraud can expand enormously in scope, speed, and devastation. In this new world, the Internet and instantaneous banking transactions make financial frauds a danger to both individuals and entire economies worldwide.

INSTITUTIONAL FRAUD

Investors generally feel secure putting their money into large, well-established, and previously reputable corporations,

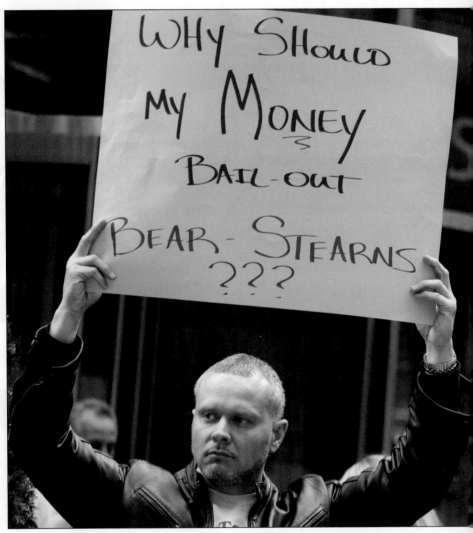

A demonstrator in New York City expresses his anger at the bailout of Wall Street investment firm Bear Stearns by the U.S. government.

investment funds, or other for-profit enterprises and financial institutions that very few would suspect of ever swindling their clients. However, it is this sometimes false sense of security and trust that has allowed millions of investors to fall victim

to large, system-wide frauds that go undetected even by supposedly hawk-eyed government regulators.

Institutional frauds are different than everyday scams because they often involve high-ranking executives (or groups of executives) playing with large pools of money. Their misuse of these funds can negatively impact not only the people invested in a company—its stockholders—but also the firm's employees, who may lose their jobs and paychecks if the directors' bad decision making leads to a reversal of the company's fortunes.

These kinds of corporate frauds are often far more complex and harder to detect than those perpetrated by a rogue, individual scammer. Even the highly skilled regulators in charge of making sure that companies are playing by the rules can miss suspicious activity and signs of trouble. Unfortunately, recent history has provided ample and dramatic examples of these kinds of corporate criminal activities and financial scandals. These include the stunning downfall of companies such as Enron and WorldCom, and the conviction and imprisonment of their executives.

WorldCom: When the Bubble Burst

In the late 1990s, there was a telecommunications, or telecom, craze in the stock market. One of the most successful telecom companies was WorldCom, founded by Bernard Ebbers. Ebbers had taken over many other telecoms throughout the 1990s. He often used WorldCom stock as payment for these companies. This put enormous pressure on WorldCom's stocks to keep rising in price in order to continue funding further acquisitions. One of these stock-funded acquisitions was MCI Communications, a surprise move in which WorldCom bought a company much larger than itself.

During this period, many telecom companies' stocks were overvalued—hence the term "telecom bubble." The prices were inflated, but there was nothing of substance causing the increased valuation. Some market analysts feared the bubble would burst, resulting in a very rapid decline in stock value, the loss of billions of dollars of investors' money, and the likelihood of many telecoms going out of business.

These analysts were right. In reality, WorldCom and other telecoms were not doing well, despite their ever-rising stock prices. It was later revealed that Ebbers and others had manipulated company figures to pretend that WorldCom was as successful as ever, if not more so. They hid actual expenses, profits, debts, and losses. The SEC also discovered that Ebbers

DAILY ◉ NEWS

NEW YORK'S HOMETOWN NEWSPAPER

Our reporter leaves home with $100 and her bathrobe. Assignment: Hit the street and GET DRESSED. Wait till you see the result!

THERSDAY SECTION PAGE 46

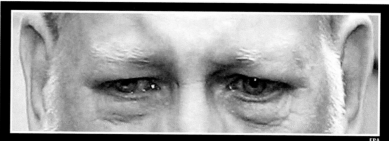

EPA

BILLION DOLLAR BABY

AP

■ WorldCom swindler Bernie Ebbers gets 25 years and weeps

■ Fleeced victims say justice is served

SEE PAGE 5

The conviction and sentencing of former WorldCom CEO Bernie Ebbers to twenty-five years in prison made the front page of the *New York Daily News* on July 14, 2005.

had borrowed $400 million from WorldCom to cover his personal debts. Ebbers was fired as chief executive officer (CEO) in April 2002. He later admitted inflating his company's value by as much as $11 billion. From a high of over $60 a share, WorldCom's stock soon fell to mere pennies. The company quickly went bankrupt. In 2005, Bernard Ebbers was sentenced to twenty-five years in prison for his financial crimes.

THE ENRON SCANDAL

In the early 2000s, it seemed a new large-scale financial fraud was exposed every few months. No downfall was as dramatic or devastating, however, as that of the former energy giant Enron. Once the nation's seventh-largest corporation, with more than twenty-one thousand employees in forty nations, Enron ran diverse businesses related to the energy markets. Its stock traded as high as $90 a share, and for years the financial media had considered it America's most innovative company.

Much like WorldCom, the reality of Enron's creatively accounted finances and dishonest activities was hidden from public and government regulatory view. One of Enron's most serious deceptions was the sale of parts of the business to shell companies, which were still secretly operated by Enron. Enron claimed a profit from these sales, while these companies, known as special purpose entities (SPEs), were used to hide Enron's massive debts and losses.

Another of Enron's tricks was to count certain business transactions purely as profit. For instance, if Enron traded $100,000 worth of energy with another company and made a $5,000 profit, it might list $105,000 as pure income. Yet

A Roll Call of Enron Victims

- **Scott and Denys Watson were two Enron employees who met at the company and married in 1998. They lost $575,000 in retirement funds and stock options when the company collapsed. Scott Watson had also started studying for a degree that the company agreed to pay for before it went bankrupt.**
- **Charlie Prestwood, a retired, thirty-three-year power plant veteran, had more than $1.3 million in retirement savings disappear.**
- **Bill Peterson, a computer specialist, was undergoing chemotherapy for his cancer when the company collapsed. He was forced to sell his house to continue paying for treatments.**
- **Dozens of charities and community organizations that depended heavily on Enron donations were negatively affected: United Way, Houston's Alley Theater, the Houston Opera, the M.D. Anderson Cancer Center, and many more.**

another tactic was something called "mark-to-market accounting," in which Enron counted what it hoped would be future profits on a project—a gas pipeline, for example—as money already earned. Much of this creative accounting was linked to chief financial officer (CFO) Andrew Fastow, while founder Kenneth Lay and CEO Jeff Skilling were partners in the fraud.

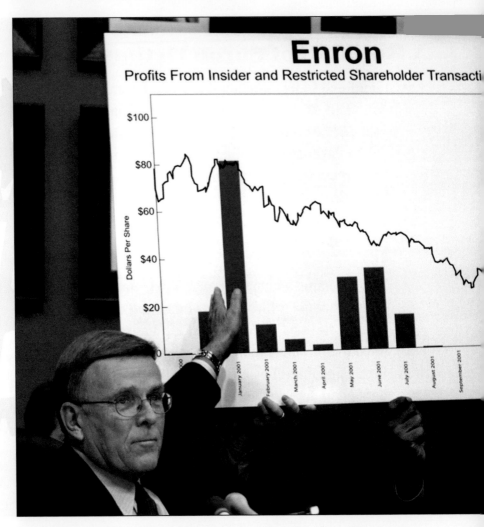

U.S. senator Byron Dorgan of North Dakota—then chairman of the Senate Commerce Committee and a critic of financial deregulation—shows a graph depicting the collapsing profits of Enron during a hearing on December 18, 2001.

Even worse, before their crimes fully came to light in late 2001, Lay, Skilling, and other executives publicly told Enron employees and other shareholders to hold on to their stocks. They assured their employees and investors that all was well,

even as they began unloading their own Enron shares, knowing that the stock price would soon collapse. There was even a thirty-day period during which the executives forbid employee shareholders from selling their shares.

Lay and Skilling left Enron well before its December 2001 declaration of bankruptcy. Fastow and Skilling eventually received heavy prison sentences. Lay died of a heart attack before he was sentenced to what many expected would have been twenty to thirty years in jail, effectively a life sentence for the then sixty-four-year-old man.

THE ENRON FALLOUT

Some of the biggest victims of the Enron accounting scandal were the vast majority of the company's law-abiding employees. In addition to losing their jobs, many lost their whole pensions in the form of Enron stock, its value having gone up in smoke nearly overnight. Among shareholders in the general public, it is believed that as much as $200 billion of value was lost.

One of the most dramatic results of the Enron fiasco was the simultaneous collapse of Arthur Andersen, Enron's accounting firm. Trusted and respected for decades, it was declared extremely negligent in allowing Enron to "cook the books." In effect, Arthur Andersen had been complicit in Enron's misleading the public about the true state of its finances. By repeatedly putting its seal of approval on Enron, Arthur Andersen encouraged the public to continue trusting

A police officer leads former Enron CEO Kenneth Lay into federal court in Houston, Texas, on July 8, 2004. Lay passed away from a heart attack in July 2006 before being sentenced for his conviction on ten counts of fraud and related charges.

and investing in a company that was losing millions of dollars every year. Arthur Andersen surrendered its accounting license in August 2002. The accounting company of eighty-five thousand people was split up and sold off.

Much of the harm caused by Enron can be chalked up to the greed and arrogance of its executives, particularly Lay, Skilling, and Fastow. In the years since the collapse of Enron, however, many observers agreed that the Wall Street system itself, along with lax government regulators and a media enthralled by Enron's global success and soaring stock prices, all created a conducive environment for rampant corporate fraud. Because of these enablers, Lay and Enron developed a reputation for brilliant, unstoppable success. Many investors, government regulators, accountants, and journalists let down their guard and gave them a free pass.

CHAPTER FOUR
FRAUDS AND SCAMS 2.0

Technology is neither good nor bad; it is how it is used, by whom, and for what purposes that makes the difference. In general, technology—in particular digital and Web-based technology—makes our daily lives easier, from doing our banking and shopping to chatting with friends and getting the latest news and reviews. Yet just as technology has made our lives immeasurably more convenient, so, too, has it made things a lot easier for criminals and scammers. Constantly improving technologies provide new and improved tools for thievery for nickel-and-dime crooks and billion-dollar bandits.

FRAUDS AND SCAMS GO HIGH-TECH

One of the things that has made individual frauds and scams far more common these days, and made institutional frauds far more destructive to so many more victims, is the way technology has affected our everyday financial dealings. Extremely

Traders are shown on the floor of the New York Stock Exchange (NYSE) during the time of the ongoing European debt crisis, one of several crises that brought heavy criticism of the financial system.

sophisticated electronic banking and investment systems allow millions of people and institutions to trade money, stocks, and goods almost instantaneously, to the tune of trillions of dollars every day.

The level of technology needed to commit even small-scale frauds and scams is available to nearly anyone with an Internet connection and a minimal amount of money. Small players have become very technologically sophisticated. Criminals can easily set up Web sites made to look like those of legitimate businesses and large, well-known corporations. With these tools, they easily dupe thousands of victims a year. Technology also helps such criminals evade capture and throw authorities off the trail.

"PHISHING"

Today, people use the Internet for much of their personal and private business. This includes social networking, online banking and bill paying, and Internet shopping. Wherever there is money involved, you can bet criminals are lurking, waiting to take advantage, even in cyberspace. A common type of online fraud is fittingly called "phishing" because the criminals cast a wide net to see who it will catch.

With phishing scams, the initial bait is often an e-mail that is not what it claims to be. The sender might pretend to be writing from the victims' bank or credit card company, their phone or Internet provider, or any other conceivable business. These vary in their level of complexity and professionalism and may or may not be targeted to clients of particular companies.

One devious touch is to use a phony but convincing facsimile of a reputable company's logo and branded designs and color schemes within their fraudulent e-mail. Embedded within the e-mail may be highlighted links. Your browser may indicate that the destination URL doesn't match the linked text. For example, the link's label may read "Go to Reputable Bank Corp.," but the link will actually take you to a fraudulent site that has nothing to do with Reputable Bank Corp. Clicking on this link might take you anywhere. If you are lucky, it only takes you to some advertisement or opens up a harmless pop-up window. If you are less lucky, you may invite malware, spyware, and viruses onto your computer that can both ransack your personal files and seize control of your computer and its operating system.

Clicking on a link from a fraudulent, phishing e-mail may also take you to another Web site to "confirm" personal information, like an account number, or it may ask you to reset a

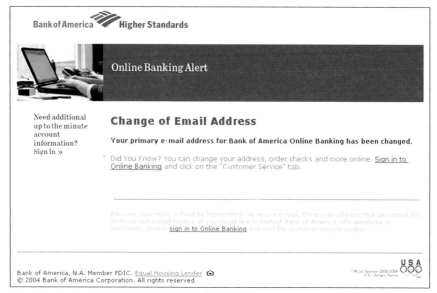

An example of a common phishing technique shows a fake e-mail sent to recipients to illegally acquire their private account data. This one was crafted to replicate a message from the well-known Bank of America.

username or password or any number of activities that could compromise your or your money's safety and expose you to identity fraud. This destination Web site might imitate the one of a legitimate company so closely that you can't tell the difference between the fake one and the real thing. Even more devious are links that redirect users to the actual, legitimate Web sites, but with the addition of a fraudulent pop-up window requesting users' personal data.

MALWARE

As already briefly mentioned, one dangerous consequence of clicking on a link in a fraudulent e-mail is the installation of sophisticated malware on your computer, which then phishes

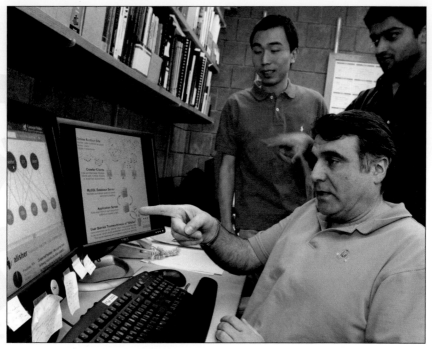

Duen Horng (*left*), Shashank Pandit (*right*), and computer science professor Christos Faloutsos (*sitting*) review antifraud software used by Internet auction sites at Carnegie Mellon University in Pittsburgh, Pennsylvania.

your system for information. Some of the malware programs hijack your e-mail accounts and send spam or phishing e-mails from your account and in your name to everyone in your address book. Other programs can lurk in your computer without your knowledge and take advantage of key-logging functions that allow thieves to spy on your keystrokes (to obtain your passwords, for example). They can also secretly scan your hard drive for documents that contain Social Security numbers, bank account information, credit card numbers, and more. At the very least, your computer could be infected with harmful viruses when you click on fraudulent links.

ONLINE AUCTION SCAMS

Some of the most popular Internet shopping tools are online auctions. Many are legitimate, such as online giant eBay.com. Many more range from the suspicious to the downright fraudulent. Common auction scams include the straightforward nondelivery fraud: you successfully bid for goods, pay for them online or via a mailed check, and never receive the promised item. Both buyers and sellers are at risk because the fraud can work both ways. You might be selling an item yourself, send the merchandise, and never receive payment.

Another danger is fake payment and money transfer services. While many auctions take advantage of legitimate payment processing services like PayPal, others are frauds. A few of these phony pay services have taken advantage of the phishing fraud described above, impersonating PayPal via e-mails and redirecting users via fraudulent links to cleverly fabricated imitations of the site. The Federal Trade Commission (FTC)

"Congratulations! You've Won!"

Yet another all-too-common e-mail scam is the one that announces that you have won a prize and now need only to claim it. While this fraud is often laughable, especially if the Web design involved is very amateur, other, more sophisticated versions have fooled even cautious victims. The culprits offer in-demand consumer items, such as an iPad or Xbox, and use techniques similar to those of phishers, even replicating the look and feel of the Web sites of famous retailers like Best Buy or Wal-Mart.

has uncovered hundreds of these frauds. Among the sites shut down was one called Premier-escrow.com, in which victims deposited payment for auctions on various items, including cars, but never received the purchased goods.

THE "BERNIE MADOFF" OF DATA THEFT

In January 2009, Princeton, New Jersey–based Heartland Payment Systems revealed it had suffered one of the largest computer security breaches in history. Hackers had simultaneously broken into Heartland and similar systems run by the supermarket chain Hannaford, the convenience store chain 7-Eleven, and the retailers JCPenny and Target. The veteran hacker mastermind behind it, Albert Gonzalez, led a team that was able to access more than 130 million credit and debit card numbers, along with the cardholders' personal data.

Gonzalez had actually been an FBI informant since 2003, helping the agency catch other hackers. While working on behalf of the FBI, however, he had also secretly led a 2007 breach of the retailer T. J. Maxx's computer system that yielded sensitive information regarding ninety-four million credit card accounts. Former federal prosecutor Scott Christie told *Computerworld* magazine in August 2009 that Gonzalez was "the Bernie Madoff of online data theft."

Though Gonzalez's hacking attacks are among the most dramatic and extensive, many more smaller-scale attacks occur every single day. Nearly every type of company, organization, public institution, government agency, and even military branch and intelligence agency has been targeted and breached. Even attacks that are quickly discovered can cost millions of dollars in legal fees and cleanup expenses.

Old-fashioned mail fraud remains a problem even in the cyberage. Donna Arthurs of Orlando, Florida, is seen here reviewing a flood of suspicious prize offers she received over just a few days.

MYTHS and FACTS

MYTH Only gullible, uneducated people fall for frauds and scams.

FACT People of every educational level and from every walk of life are potential victims of frauds and scams. Many skeptical, shrewd people have been taken advantage of by scam artists.

MYTH Someone who avoids shady business proposals or suspicious people is 100 percent safe from being exposed to frauds and scams.

FACT No one is completely safe. Stock speculators, hackers, and identity thieves can often defraud their victims without establishing direct contact, especially with the aid of technology.

MYTH If my identity is stolen and used for illegal purposes, it is easy to simply explain my innocence and clear the problem up.

FACT Clearing your name may be the easiest step, but untangling the damage done by identity theft can often be extremely difficult, time-consuming, stressful, and expensive.

CHAPTER FIVE

FIGHTING FINANCIAL FRAUDS AND SCAMS

In attempting to protect yourself against financial frauds and scams, you must realize that there is no way to be 100 percent safe. Sometimes even the government, its regulators, and highly intelligent observers are caught unaware and victimized by financial frauds and scams.

But fear not! You can arm yourself by being prepared, vigilant, and aware of what to look out for. Following some basic and common-sense ground rules regarding how you react to requests for information, secure your computer and other personal effects, and respond to unsolicited offers and "opportunities" can go a long way toward ensuring that you stay safe in a dangerous world. While realizing that you can't prepare for every single contingency, you can do your best to protect yourself from financial frauds and scams and limit your exposure to them.

ALWAYS ASK QUESTIONS

Whether you are contacted by phone, in person, or via e-mail, criminals always hope to take advantage of you by making you act before you realize that a fraud or scam is occurring. By slowing down the process and asking for contact information so that you can get back to the salesperson or inquire about the details of a proposition, you will almost always discourage potential thieves from continuing their correspondence with you. Insisting that you act immediately, avoiding your questions, or other shifty and pushy behaviors are a good sign that the other person is hiding something and should not be trusted.

Legitimate salespeople or charity representatives should always be willing to provide the following information: their name, the name of their business or institution, telephone number, street address, Web site, and business license number. All of this information is easily verified via the Internet or other sources, including the Better Business Bureau and government antifraud watchdog agencies. If the person cannot wait for you to get back to him or her after checking out the organization or considering the proposition carefully, there is something

wrong. In addition, a business or charity will almost never offer to pick up cash or checks by sending a messenger to your home. If someone offers to do that, cease communication immediately and give out no further personal information. Then contact law enforcement authorities.

Always be alert and ask questions if you receive any request for money over the phone. Scammers are especially eager to take advantage of youth and inexperience to cheat people out of their money or engage in identity theft.

Do Your Research

Even if you do convince a caller to give you the information you need to verify his or her legitimacy, there is always the chance that someone has provided you with false or misleading information. Again, the Internet is a valuable tool. A normal-looking Web site, address, and phone number are no guarantee that the enterprise is legitimate, especially if you have never heard of it. When in doubt, online searches can help dig up information on frauds, especially if others have already been victimized by them.

An FBI Web page (www.fbi.gov) offers helpful information on identity theft. The FBI, along with other federal agencies, provides great online resources for protecting yourself from frauds and scams.

Organizations such as the FBI, the FTC, and your local and national Better Business Bureau (BBB), an organization that helps protect consumers and tracks fraud, are great resources. You can search their Web sites to gather information on businesses and organizations or to report suspected fraudulent and criminal practices. Their Web sites also feature sections where you can gain further tips on how to identify frauds and protect yourself from them.

Finally, by Googling frauds and scams, you can access thousands of local, national, and international news articles, many of which contain valuable details that you might recognize from your contact with suspicious persons. Local news stories might be especially useful because many scam artists operate only in specific areas.

Listen to Your Suspicions

In order to allay their customers' and clients' concerns about fraud, most legitimate companies and organizations, large and small, now have policies that prohibit calling or contacting their clients directly, unless it is an emergency.

Even if you do receive correspondence from an organization or company—such as a bank, charity, or credit card company—with whom you do business regularly, it is almost unheard of that any representative will ask you to confirm your debit card, credit card, or bank account numbers. Nor will representatives ask you to confirm an entire Social Security number over the phone or via e-mail. Instead, to verify your identity, many legitimate companies will ask you to answer personal security questions whose answers you supplied to them when opening an account, like your mother's maiden name, your paternal

Sinking an Internet Phisher

Internet phishers count on us making decisions too quickly, before really thinking them through and noticing any irregularities. Look before you click on a link. It might not redirect you where you think it will. In addition, expand any e-mails to carefully examine the sender's e-mail address and the "reply-to" e-mail address. Often there will be something a bit off about any or all of these.

Imagine that you open a bank account in person, with the help of a bank officer named Mr. John Johnson at National Bank. You note that his e-mail address is jjohnson@nationalbank.com. Months later, you get a questionable e-mail disguised to look as if it came from National Bank. The e-mail might be from john.johnson@national-bank-service.com, or something similar. If the e-mail address differs from the one you were given in person by Mr. Johnson, call the bank and see if the e-mail was legitimate and if Mr. Johnson's e-mail address has indeed changed.

grandmother's first name, the name of your first pet, or the name of the street you grew up on. If you are contacted and asked to provide Social Security, credit card, or bank account numbers, ask yourself, "Is this really the bank calling me?"

In addition, when confronted with offers of prizes, easy money, or cheap goods and services, ask yourself, "How reliable are these people? Is this too good to be true?" Chances are, it probably is.

GUARD YOUR PERSONAL DATA

Any bank or other institution that provides online access to customer accounts or other personal data, including free e-mail accounts, uses data encryption technology. Computer code written into the interface between your computer and the bank's system protects you from anyone who might try to spy on your transactions or hack into your personal and financial data. The visual indicator that encryption is active usually includes an icon in the form of a lock. In addition to checking for this icon, you should also carefully read the institution's encryption policies and practices, along with its privacy guidelines.

You have control of your own privacy and personal data. But you also should ensure that any companies or organizations you deal with also have your best interests always in mind. Be sure to thoroughly check the privacy policies of any service you subscribe to, including social networks, photo-sharing Web sites, travel sites, newsletters and blogs, music and video sharing, streaming, and downloading sites. Make sure that they provide proper protection and do not sell your information to other parties. It is always preferable to have less of your data "out there" than more. Plus, you will probably receive less spam if your digital footprint remains small.

While keeping safe online, remember to do the same in your everyday life. Make sure any receipts or paperwork that include account numbers, credit card numbers, your Social Security number, and other sensitive personal data are safely hidden. If you need to throw anything away, be sure to rip it up thoroughly or run it through a paper shredder. Criminals comb through garbage because so many people dispose of these

Philip McKelroy (*foreground*) dumps old papers ready for shredding as part of Cadence Bank's Community Shred Day in Memphis, Tennessee. This is an event geared to promote recycling and proper disposal of private data to prevent identity theft.

things carelessly. Always keep careful track of any cards, including driver's licenses or passports. Report loss or theft as soon as possible. Once a credit card or driver's license expires and a new one has been obtained, destroy the old one by cutting it into pieces before throwing it away.

Another important step is keeping close track of your records. If you have a bank or credit card account, check it regularly, whether online or via phone, to make sure every charge on it makes sense to you. Criminals depend on victims waiting too long to discover suspicious charges or withdrawals. Contact your financial institution if anything seems wrong. If you use a credit card, you can easily request credit reports on a regular basis from the three major companies that provide these: Equifax, Experian, and TransUnion. This is especially useful if an account has been opened using your Social Security number but under a different name.

What If You Are the Victim of Identity Theft?

If you do discover that you have become a victim of identity theft, you need to work fast to reverse the damage. A first step is to file an Identity Theft Report, which you can do with the FTC. Take the name, contact information, and ID number of the person filing the report. Request a copy of the report via mail or e-mail because you may need it. Also contact the police to file and receive a copy of a crime report.

Another vital step is to contact the three credit reporting agencies mentioned above. They can issue an initial fraud

Local authorities work hard to educate citizens about frauds and scams. Displayed here are printed materials about identity theft from the Albuquerque, New Mexico, attorney general's office.

alert that shows your credit may have been compromised. This is also a good idea if you lose or have your data or documents stolen but have not noticed any suspicious activity yet. If you have become a victim of credit fraud or identity theft, the agencies might require a police report. It can then issue a "letter of clearance," which officially states that your case has been confirmed as identity theft. This is important in case creditors—anyone you owe money to, such as a bank or credit card company—contact you trying to collect on charges and purchases made by the person who has stolen your personal and financial information.

Finally, when dealing with any authorities, credit agencies, or your own creditors, always request copies of any and all forms, reports, and written correspondence, and save your e-mails to and from these authorities, agencies, and representatives, just to be safe.

Look Before You Leap

Less straightforward is staying safe from wide-scale and institutional fraud. Most of the victims of the Madoff and Enron scandals, for example, were not to blame for the dishonest actions of their victimizers. Many politicians, activists, and regulators have called for tougher rules and regulations governing businesses and the financial markets, and the struggle to keep up with new types of frauds continues.

However, many of the same tips that protect us from common scams also apply to the stock market and other forms of financial speculation. Before investing in stocks or making any other kind of financial transaction, do extensive research. Ignore pumped-up and feel-good news coverage of companies or investment ideas, and examine how similar enterprises have worked out in the past. If you have the money to invest, you should seek out a trusted—and independent—financial adviser.

Also, be suspicious of results that are too good to be true. Both Madoff's victims and those in the Enron and WorldCom scandals were too eager to look the other way, even though some basic research may have tipped them off that these were suspicious propositions. The same was true many years ago for Charles Ponzi's victims. In many cases, if an investment scheme is so complicated that even some of the best and brightest financial experts, accountants, and regulators cannot really explain how it works, chances are it is not the safest investment.

Staying informed is one of your greatest defenses against frauds and scams. Educating yourself on how criminals operate directly and indirectly will help you and your family remain safe. Having realistic expectations for deals and returns on investment will help, too. We have seen how hopes for a quick payoff and easy money sometimes make potential victims blind to frauds and scams. Even many extremely smart and savvy citizens fall victim precisely because they do not think it can happen to them. Well-known blue-chip corporations and highly regarded financial analysts can be defrauded, and government and enforcement agencies have sometimes failed to protect the public. In the end, understanding and protecting against financial frauds and scams begins and ends with only one person—you!

Ten Great Questions
to Ask a Financial Adviser

1 How can I check whether a business proposal or investment opportunity is indeed legitimate?

2 If it is legitimate, is this particular investment low-risk, medium-risk, or high-risk?

3 How can I make sure that a trusted investment firm is making the right decisions about my money?

4 I have never heard of the charity that is asking me for money. How do I make sure it is legitimate?

5 Where can I check to see if a particular business has a clean record in dealing with its clients/customers?

6 What are some of the worst consequences of having your identity stolen? How can I best protect my personal information, especially online?

7 How do I go about recovering my lost savings after being the victim of a fraud or clearing my name after an instance of identity theft?

8 What are the best organizations that work to combat financial frauds and scams?

9 How and to whom do I report suspected or actual fraudulent activity?

10 How effective have local, state, and federal law enforcement agencies been in catching financial scammers?

GLOSSARY

advance fee fraud A type of fraud in which the victim is tricked into paying money up front to realize a greater financial gain in the future.

bubble A period of intense financial speculation, or boom, in a particular industry, followed by a downturn, in which the bubble bursts; a bubble is often marked by dramatic rises and falls in stock prices.

con Short for "confidence game" or "confidence trick"; a type of fraud in which the criminal gains the confidence of the victim before robbing or defrauding him or her.

con man Short for "confidence man"; a person (male or female) who specializes in confidence games or tricks (in gaining the confidence of their victims before robbing or defrauding them).

encryption Security software that allows safe transmission of private data between users and outside networks, usually via the Internet.

Federal Trade Commission (FTC) An agency of the federal government that regulates business practices, including investigating and prosecuting frauds and scams.

419 scam A type of advance-fee scam in which the victim is defrauded in the process of attempting to secure a promised, yet nonexistent, sum of money, usually located overseas.

hacker A computer programmer who specializes in illegally invading secure computer networks.

identity theft A type of fraud in which the personal data of a victim is used by a criminal to impersonate him or her with the ultimate goal of illegal financial gain.

malware Unwanted software secretly installed on a person's computer via the Internet; the victim's computer can then be programmed for malicious purposes.

mark Slang term for a victim of a con game or other fraud or scam.

mark-to-market A type of accounting practice in which future, expected profits are counted as ones already earned.

money laundering The process of depositing money made by illegal means into a bank or other financial institution, thereby concealing its criminal origins.

mortgage loan A loan provided to someone for the purpose of purchasing a home.

Nigerian letter Another term for a 419 scam (which may originate in any nation).

phishing A type of e-mail fraud in which someone attempts to obtain private data from an e-mail recipient by posing as a trustworthy party.

Ponzi scheme Named after Charles Ponzi; a type of fraud in which initial investors are paid from the contributions of later ones, but in which no actual investments are made and no new wealth is generated.

pyramid scheme A type of fraud, similar to a Ponzi scheme, in which the only money made is by enlisting others into the scheme and forcing them to pay to join; their payments move up the line of "investors," who take a

percentage of it but pass the bulk up to those above
them. A pyramid scheme primarily enriches only the
person or group of individuals at the very top.

returns Profits made on an investment, sometimes referred to
as interest.

special purpose entity (SPE) A company created by another
company for a special purpose, such as hiding debt or
limiting financial risk.

telecom Short for "telecommunications"; a company engaged
in business related to mobile phones, landlines, and
computer network infrastructure.

FOR MORE INFORMATION

Better Business Bureau (BBB)
4200 Wilson Boulevard, Suite 800
Arlington, VA 22203-1838
(703) 276-0100
Web site: http://www.bbb.org
The BBB, with individual branches throughout the United
States and Canada, is dedicated to ensuring corporate
responsibility and fair business practices.

Canadian Anti-Fraud Centre
Box 686
North Bay, ON P1B 8J8
Canada
(888) 495-8501
Web site: http://www.phonebusters.com
The Canadian Anti-Fraud Centre provides resources for
recognizing and fighting common frauds and scams.

Family Online Safety Institute (FOSI)
815 Connecticut Avenue, Suite 220
Washington, DC 20006
(202) 572-6252
Web site: http://www.fosi.org

The FOSI is an international, nonprofit organization that
works to develop a safer Internet for children and
families. It works to influence public policies and educate
the public.

Federal Bureau of Investigation (FBI)
935 Pennsylvania Avenue NW
Washington, DC 20535-0001
(202) 324-3000
Web site: http://www.fbi.gov
The FBI, as part of its mandate as the top federal law enforcement agency, investigates financial frauds and cybercrime,
such as Internet fraud and identity theft.

Federal Trade Commission (FTC)
600 Pennsylvania Avenue NW
Washington, DC 20580
(202) 326-2222
Web site: http://www.ftc.gov
The FTC is a U.S. federal agency with the power to investigate various consumer complaints, including dishonest
business practices, frauds, and scams.

Get Net Wise
Internet Education Foundation
1634 I Street NW
Washington, DC 20009
Web site: http://www.getnetwise.org
Get Net Wise is part of the Internet Education Foundation,
which works to provide a safe online environment for
children and families.

Internet Keep Safe Coalition
1401 K Street NW, Suite 600
Washington, DC 20005
(866) 794-7233
Web site: http://www.ikeepsafe.org
The Internet Keep Safe Coalition is an educational resource
    for children and families that educates about Internet
    safety and ethics associated with Internet technologies.

i-SAFE Inc.
5900 Pasteur Court, Suite #100
Carlsbad, CA 92008
(760) 603-7911
Web site: http://www.isafe.org
Founded in 1998, i-SAFE Inc., is the leader in Internet safety
    education. Available in all fifty states, Washington, D.C.,
    and Department of Defense schools across the world,
    i-SAFE is a nonprofit foundation whose mission is to
    educate and empower youth to make their Internet experi-
    ences safe and responsible. The goal is to educate students
    on how to avoid dangerous, inappropriate, or unlawful
    online behavior.

Royal Canadian Mounted Police (RCMP)
Headquarters Building
1200 Vanier Parkway
Ottawa, ON K1A 0R2
Canada
(613) 993-7267
Web site: http://www.rcmp-grc.gc.ca/scams-fraudes/
    index-eng.htm.

The RCMP is Canada's federal law enforcement agency, with the power to investigate various types of fraud, including online fraud.

U.S. Securities and Exchange Commission (SEC)
100 F Street NE
Washington, DC 20549
(202) 942-8088
Web site: http://www.sec.gov
The SEC is the primary federal government agency that regulates the financial markets.

WEB SITES

Due to the changing nature of Internet links, Rosen Publishing has developed an online list of Web sites related to the subject of this book. This site is updated regularly. Please use this link to access the list:

http://www.rosenlinks.com/rwe/fraud

FOR FURTHER READING

Anderson, Dale, and Sabrina Crewe. *The FBI and White-Collar Crime*. Broomall, PA: Mason Crest Publishers, 2010.

Hanel, Richard. *Identity Theft* (Controversy!). Salt Lake City, UT: Benchmark Books, 2010.

Kiesbye, Stefan. *Identity Theft* (At Issue Series). Farmington Hills, MI: Greenhaven Press, 2011.

Marzilli, Alan. *The Internet and Crime* (Point/Counterpoint). New York, NY: Chelsea House, 2009.

Mooney, Carla. *Online Security* (Issues in the Digital Age). San Diego, CA: Referencepoint Press, 2011.

Nardo, Don. *Bernie Madoff* (People in the News). Farmington Hills, MI: Lucent Books, 2011.

Ross, Jeffrey Ian. *Cybercrime* (Criminal Investigations). New York, NY: Chelsea House, 2009.

Vacca, John, Mary E. Vacca, and Marc Rogers. *Identity Theft* (Cybersafety). New York, NY: Chelsea House, 2011.

Young, Mitchell. *White Collar Crime* (Issues on Trial). Farmington Hills, MI: Greenhaven Press, 2009.

BIBLIOGRAPHY

Alt, Betty L., and Sandra K. Wells. *Fleecing Grandma and Grandpa: Protecting Against Scams, Cons, and Frauds.* Westport, CT: Praeger, 2004.

Altman, Alex. "A Brief History of Ponzi Schemes." *Time*, December 15, 2008. Retrieved October 2011 (http://www.time.com/time/business/article/0,8599,1866680,00.html).

Arnall, Dan. "WorldCom at a Glance." *ABC News*, March 15, 2005. Retrieved October 2011 (http://abcnews.go.com/Business/story?id=582962&page=1#.TsNHMj3NltM).

Better Business Bureau. "Work at Home Schemes." Retrieved October 2011 (http://www.bbb.org/us/article/work-at-home-schemes-408).

Chew, Robert. "Madoff's Victims: Finding Meaning in the Devastation." *Time*, December 30, 2008. Retrieved October 2011 (http://www.time.com/time/business/article/0,8599,1869043,00.html).

Cohn, Scott. "Some Enron Victims Still Trying to Recover." MSNBC.com, May 26, 2006. Retrieved October 2011 (http://www.msnbc.msn.com/id/12976443/ns/business-cnbc_tv/t/some-enron-victims-still-trying-recover/#.TsrOez3NltM).

Dignan, Larry. "Beware the Delta Airlines Phishing Attack." ZDNet.com, November 16, 2011. Retrieved November

2011 (http://www.zdnet.com/blog/btl/beware-the-delta-air-lines-phishing-attack/63608).

Di Stefano, Theodore F. "WorldCom's Failure: Why Did It Happen?" *E-Commerce Times*, August 19, 2005. Retrieved October 2011 (http://www.ecommercetimes.com/story/45542.html).

Economist. "The Madoff Affair: Con of the Century." December 18, 2008. Retrieved October 2011 (http://www.economist.com/node/12818310).

FBI.gov. "Internet Fraud." Retrieved October 2011 (http://www.fbi.gov/scams-safety/fraud/internet_fraud).

Fontinelle, Amy. "What to Do If Your Identity Is Stolen." *San Francisco Chronicle*, November 18, 2011. Retrieved November 2011 (http://www.sfgate.com/cgi-bin/article.cgi?f=/g/a/2011/11/18/investopedia65743.DTL).

FTC Press Release. "Internet Auction Fraud Targeted by Law Enforcers." April 30, 2003. Retrieved October 2011 (http://www.ftc.gov/opa/2003/04/bidderbeware.shtm).

Gaudin, Sharon. "Government Informant Is Called Kingpin of Largest U.S. Data Breaches." *Computerworld*, August 18, 2009. Retrieved October 2009 (http://www.computerworld.com/s/article/9136787/Government_informant_is_called_kingpin_of_largest_U.S._data_breaches).

Gaviria, Marcela, and Martin Smith. "The Madoff Affair." *PBS Frontline*, May 2009. Retrieved October 2011 (http://www.pbs.org/wgbh/pages/frontline/madoff).

Goodier, Robert. "Villalobos Investors Hold Government Responsible." *Tico Times*, November 4, 2005. Retrieved October 2011 (http://www.explorecostarica.com/newsmanager/publish/article_804.shtml).

Hall, Matthew T., and John Marelius. "Ponzi Schemer Dominelli's Death News to San Diego." *San Diego Union-Tribune*, October 14, 2009. Retrieved October 2011 (http://www.signonsandiego.com/news/2009/oct/14/ponzi-schemer-dominellis-death-news-san-diego).

Henderson, Les. *Crimes of Persuasion: Schemes, Scams, Frauds.* Azilda, ON, Canada: Coyote Ridge Publishing, 2003.

Jordan, Bob. "Ponzi Scheme Hit N.J. Investors, Officials Say." *Asbury Park Press*, November 7, 2011. Retrieved November 2011 (http://www.app.com/article/20111108/NJBIZ/311080020/Ponzi-scheme-hit-N-J-investors-officials-say).

Kaplan, David. "Faces of Enron: The Watsons—Enron Couple Loses $575,000." *Houston Chronicle*, December 9, 2001. Retrieved October 2011 (http://www.chron.com/CDA/archives/archive.mpl/2001_3355152/the-faces-of-enron-the-watsons-enron-couple-lose-5.html).

Leek, Gordon G. *Trust Me: Frauds, Schemes, and How to Avoid Them.* Toronto, ON, Canada: Dundurn, 2010.

Levinson, Meredith. "Why Law Enforcement Can't Stop Hackers." *PC World*, November 16, 2011. Retrieved November 2011 (http://www.pcworld.com/businesscenter/article/244057/why_law_enforcement_cant_stop_hackers.html).

Matulich, Serge, and David M. Currie, eds. *Handbook of Frauds, Scams, and Swindles: Failures of Ethics in Leadership.* Boca Raton, FL: CRC Press, 2008.

O'Donnell, Jayne, and Jillian Berman. "Work-at-Home Jobs Scams Thrive on Economic Trouble." *USA Today*, July 1, 2010. Retrieved October 2011 (http://www.usatoday

.com/money/economy/employment/2010-06-29-workathome29_CV_N.htm).

Ove, Torsten. "Investment Operation in Costa Rica Took in Hundreds of Millions; Then It All Fell Apart." *Pittsburgh Post-Gazette*, May 11, 2003. Retrieved October 2011 (http://www.post-gazette.com/localnews/20030511thebrothers0511p5.asp).

PBS Newshour. "Enron Update." January 28, 2002. Retrieved October 2011 (http://www.pbs.org/newshour/bb/business/jan-june02/enron_1-28.html).

Robinson, Jeffrey. *There's a Sucker Born Every Minute: A Revelation of Audacious Frauds, Scams, and Cons—How to Spot Them, How to Stop Them*. New York, NY: Perigree Trade, 2002.

Saporito, Bill. "How Fastow Helped Enron Fall." *Time*, February 10, 2002. Retrieved October 2011 (http://www.time.com/time/business/article/0,8599,201871,00.html).

Sarna, David E. Y. *History of Greed: Financial Fraud from Tulip Mania to Bernie Madoff*. Hoboken, NJ: Wiley, 2010.

Smith, Hedrick, and Marc Shaffer. "Bigger Than Enron." *Frontline*, June 20, 2002. Retrieved October 2011 (http://www.pbs.org/wgbh/pages/frontline/shows/regulation).

Smith, Hedrick, and Rick Young. "The Wall Street Fix." *Frontline*, May 22, 2003. Retrieved October 2011 (http://www.pbs.org/wgbh/pages/frontline/shows/wallstreet).

Sunseri, Gina. "Enron Victims Look Forward to Justice at Trial." *ABC News*, January 30, 2006. Retrieved November 2011 (http://abcnews.go.com/Business/LegalCenter/story?id=1556334&page=1#.TsrWnT3NltM).

Swierczynski, Duane. *The Complete Idiot's Guide to Frauds, Scams, and Cons.* Indianapolis, IN: Alpha, 2002.

Tynan, Dan. "Top Five Online Scams." *PC World*, March 9, 2005. Retrieved October 2011 (http://www.pcworld .com/article/119941/top_five_online_scams.html).

USA Today. "The Enron Scandal by the Numbers." January 21, 2002. Retrieved November 2011 (http://www.usatoday. com/money/energy/2002-01-22-enron-numbers.htm).

USA Today. "Enron Who's Who." January 26, 2006. Retrieved November 2011 (http://www.usatoday.com/money/ industries/energy/2006-01-26-enron-whos-who_x.htm#).

USA Today. "Timeline of the Tyco International Scandal." June 17, 2005. Retrieved October 2011 (http://www .usatoday.com/money/industries/manufacturing/2005- 06-17-tyco-timeline_x.htm#).

Vijayan, Jaikumar. "Heartland Breach Shows Why Compliance Is Not Enough." *Computerworld*, January 6, 2010. Retrieved October 2011 (http://www. computerworld.com/s/article/9143158/Update_ Heartland_breach_shows_why_compliance_is_ not_enough).

Wearden, Graeme, and Nick Mathiason. "Famous Names Pepper Madoff Client List." *Guardian*, February 5, 2009. Retrieved October 2011 (http://www.guardian.co.uk/ business/2009/feb/05/madoff-client-list).

INDEX

About the Author

Philip Wolny is the author of another economics-related book entitled *How Debt and Default Affect You*, from Rosen Publishing's Your Economic Future series. He is grateful that his closest encounters with actual financial frauds and scams have been limited to the bad grammar and improbable claims of the various 419 letters he receives in his inbox. He hopes to keep it that way. Wolny is from Queens, New York.

Photo Credits

Cover (scandal) © istockphoto.com/Lilli Day; cover and interior graphics (graph) © istockphoto.com/Andrey Prokhorov; cover, p. 1 (gavel) © istockphoto.com/Don Bayley; p. 6 Spencer Platt/Getty Images; p. 9 Kim Steele/Photodisc/Getty Images; pp. 14–15, 35 NY Daily News Archive/Getty Images; pp. 16, 18–19, 40, 46 © AP Images; p. 22 Pictorial Parade/Archive Photos/Getty Images; p. 24 © Jerry Rife/The San Diego Union/ZUMA Press; p. 26 Hulteng KRT/Newscom; p. 30 Timothy A. Clary/AFP/Getty Images; pp. 32–33, 43 Bloomberg/Getty Images; pp. 38–39 Kevin Lamarque/Reuters/Landov; p. 45 © Zoriah/ZUMA Press; p. 49 KRT/Newscom; pp. 52–53 Jupiterimages/Goodshoot/Thinkstock; pp. 58–59 © Jim Weber/The Commercial Appeal/ZUMA Press; p. 60 © Dean Hanson/Journal/Albuquerque Journal/ZUMA Press; interior graphics (people) © istockphoto.com/studiovision; interior graphics (side arrows) © istockphoto.com/Darja Tokranova; interior graphics (cogs) © istockphoto.com/Chan Fu Soh; interior graphics (circled arrows) © istockphoto.com/articular; back cover and interior graphics (up arrows) © istockphoto.com/Dean Turner.

Designer: Michael Moy; Photo Researcher: Amy Feinberg